Easy Trombone S

Contents

3901

Beautiful Isle Of Somewhere

JOHN S. FEARIS

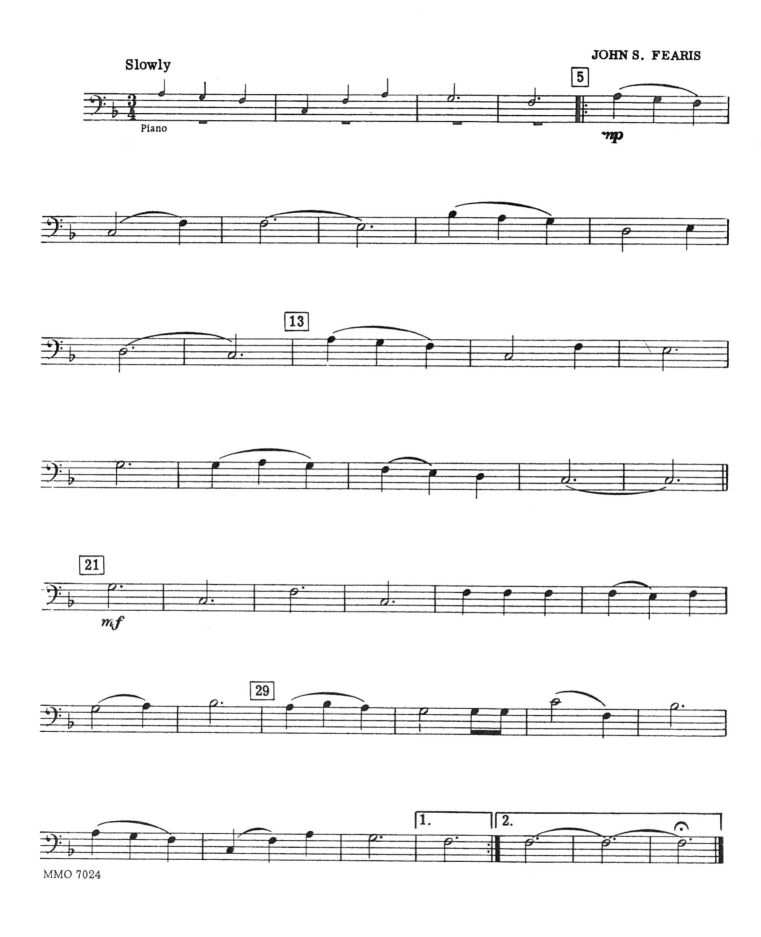

To A Wild Rose

4 beats (2 measures)
precede music.

EDWARD MAC DOWELL, Op. 51

With simple tenderness

Daisy Bell

HARRY DACRE

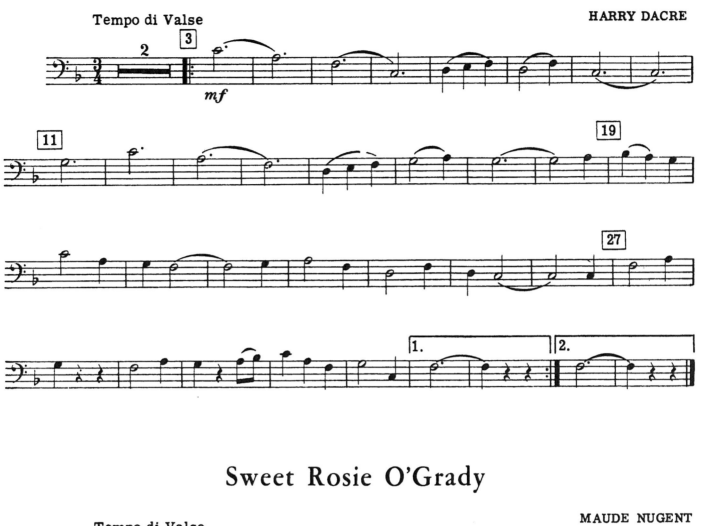

Sweet Rosie O'Grady

MAUDE NUGENT

Pomp And Circumstance

5

EDWARD ELGAR

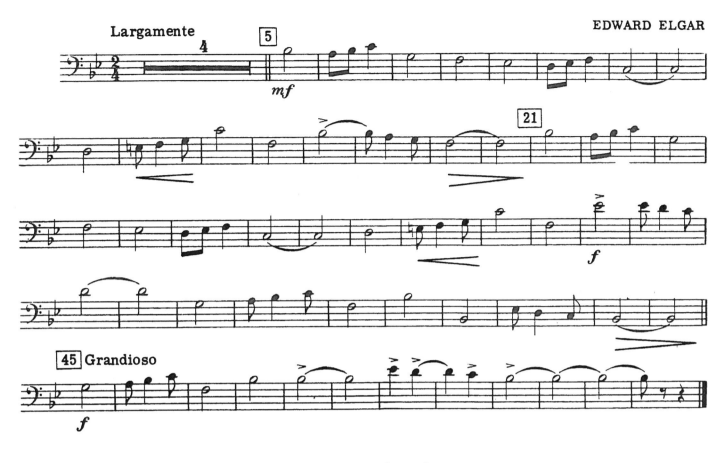

Mighty Lak' A Rose

ETHELBERT NEVIN

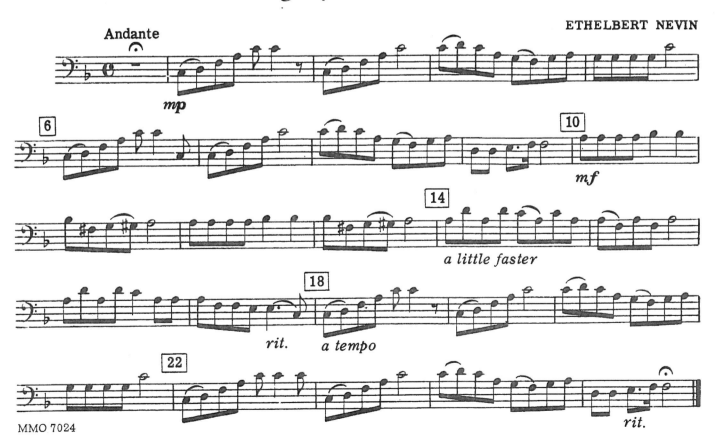

MMO 7024

Kentucky Babe

ADAM GEIBEL

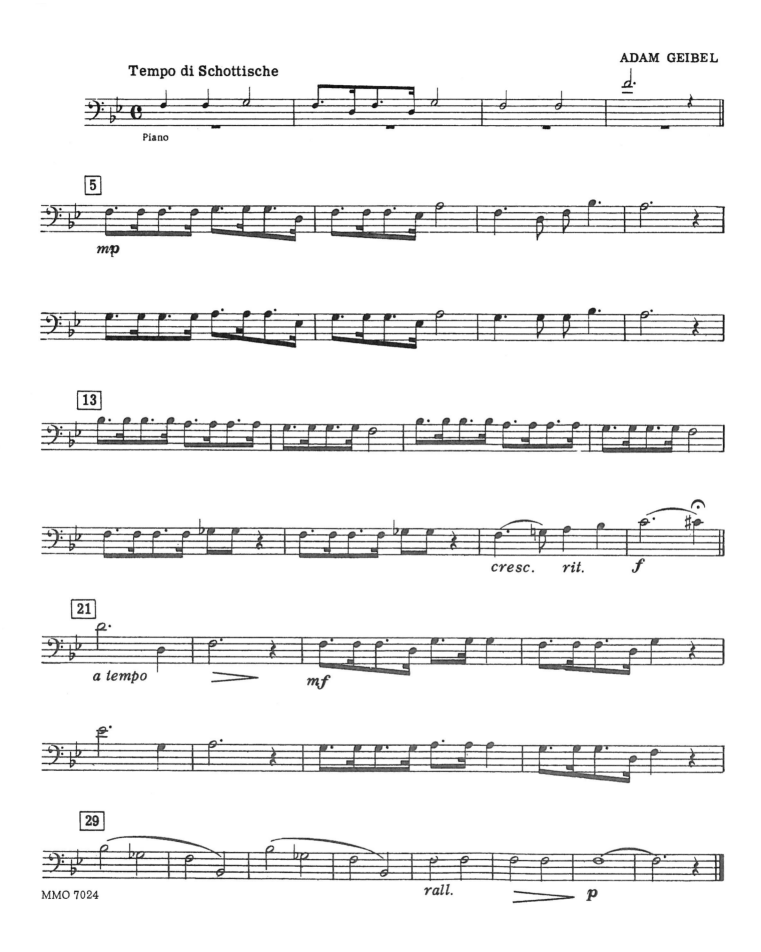

The Band Played On

Tempo di Valse   CHARLES E. WARD

MMO 7024

After The Ball

CHARLES K. HARRIS

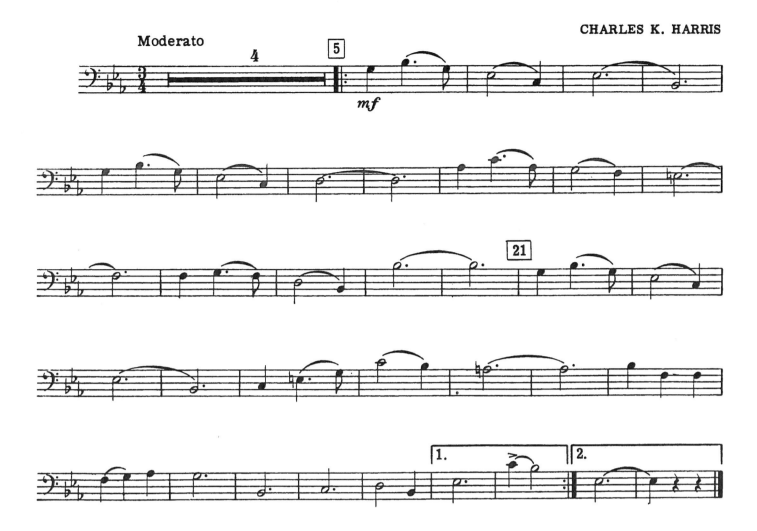

Santa Lucia

Neapolitan Song

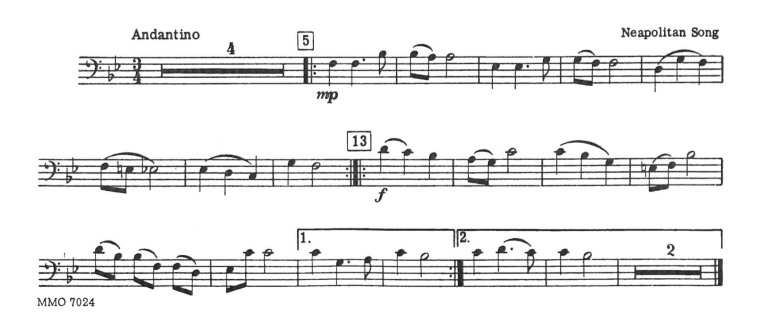

Red River Valley

Slowly

Cowboy Song

Kathleen Mavourneen

Andante

FREDERICK N. CROUCH

America, The Beautiful

3 beats (3/4 measure)
precede music.

KATHERINE LEE BATES
SAMUEL A. WARD

Grandioso

Hatikvoh

(The Hope)

Hebrew National Anthem

4 beats (1 measure)
precede music.

Moderato

MMO 7024

American Patrol

Tempo di Marcia

F. W. MEACHAM

3 beats plus 1 silent precede music.

Battle Hymn Of The Republic

JULIA WARD HOWE

Moderato

MMO 7024

I'll Sing Thee Songs Of Araby

FREDERIC CLAY

Andantino

In Old Madrid

Tempo di Bolero

H. TROTERE

O Sole Mio!

Andante

E. DI CAPUA

La Paloma

Andante

SEBASTIAN YRADIER

MMO 7024

La Spagnola

3 beats (1 measure)
precede music.

VINCENZO DI CHIARA

Tempo di Valse

MMO 7024

La Cumparsita

4 beats (2 measures)
precede music.

G. H. MATOS RODRIGUEZ

MMO 7024

Adios Muchachos

CARLOS SANDERS

El Choclo

A. G. VILLOLDO

Oh Promise Me

REGINALD DE KOVEN

Because

GUY D'HARDELOT

The Rosary

4 beats (1 measure)
precede music.

ETHELBERT NEVIN

MMO 7024

Just A-Wearyin' For You

CARRIE JACOBS-BOND

I Love You Truly

CARRIE JACOBS-BOND

MMO 7024

Vilia

Moderato

FRANZ LEHAR

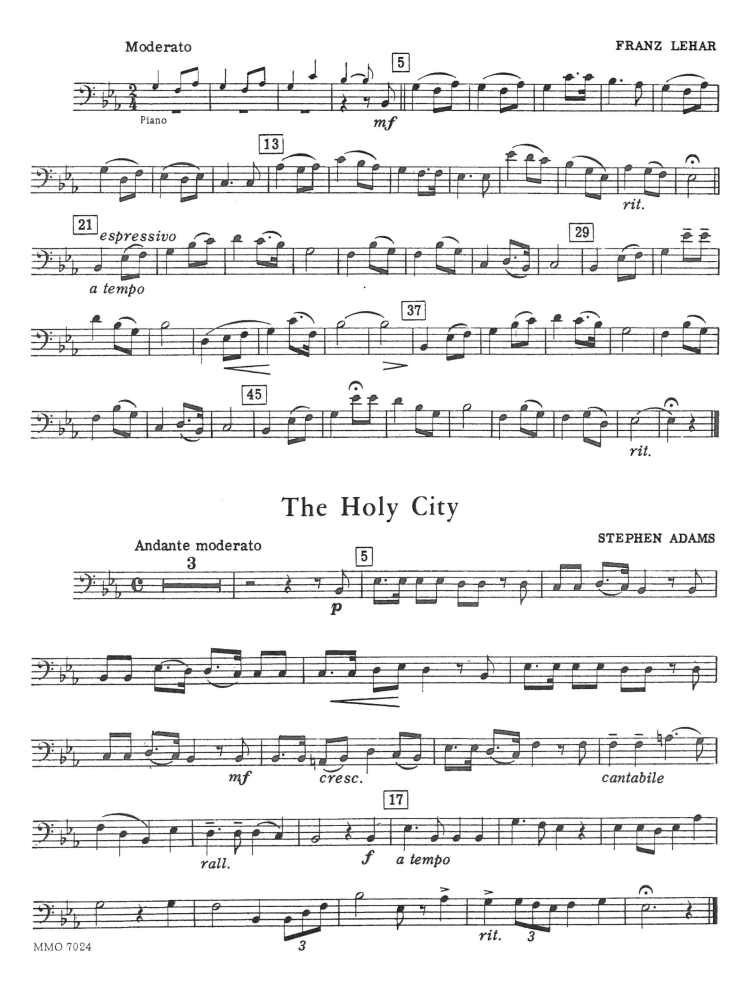

The Holy City

Andante moderato

STEPHEN ADAMS

Gypsy Love Song

VICTOR HERBERT

Slowly

rit.   a tempo.   rit.

Marche Slave

P. I. TSCHAIKOWSKY, Op. 31

Moderato   *3 espressivo*

Ah! So Pure

FRIEDRICH VON FLOTOW

Eili, Eili

Hebrew Melody

3 beats (1 measure)
precede music.

Who Is Sylvia?

FRANZ SCHUBERT

Theme

(from Piano Concerto, Op. 16)

EDVARD GRIEG

Song Of India

Andantino

N. RIMSKY-KORSAKOFF

Serenade

Andante grazioso

VICTOR HERBERT

Finlandia

Andante sostenuto

JEAN SIBELIUS

Theme

(from Piano Concerto No. 2, Op. 18)

SERGEI RACHMANINOFF

Moderato

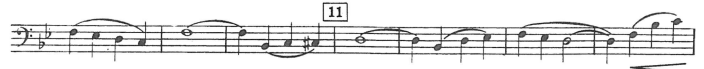

Für Elise

5 beats plus 4 soft beats
(3 meas.) precede music.

LUDWIG VAN BEETHOVEN

Fantasie Impromptu

(Theme)

FREDERIC CHOPIN, Op. 66

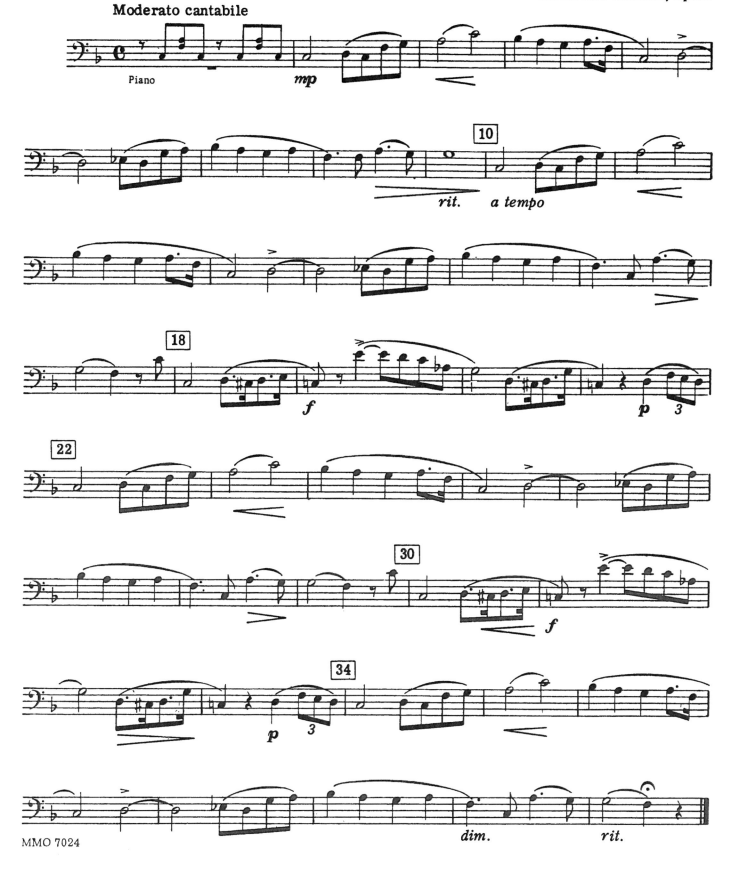

Mexican Hat Dance

4 beats (2 measures)
set tempo.

F. A. PARTICHELA

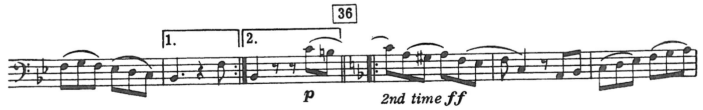

The Glow Worm

PAUL LINCKE

Trombone

Chamber Classics

Baroque Brass and Beyond: Quintets	MMO CD 3904	$29.98
Classical Trombone Solos	MMO CD 3909	$29.98
Music for Brass Ensemble	MMO CD 3905	$29.98
Sticks & Bones: Brass Quintets	MMO CD 3927	$29.98
STRAVINSKY L'Histoire du Soldat	MMO CD 3908	$29.98

Inspirational Classics

Christmas Memories	MMO CDG 1203	$19.98

Instrumental Classics with Orchestra

Band Aids: Concert Band Favorites	MMO CD 3930	$29.98
Popular Concert Favorites w/Orch.	MMO CD 3929	$29.98

Jazz, Standards and Big Band

2+2=5: A Study Odd Times	MMO CD 2044	$19.98
Bacharach Revisited	MMO CD 3974	$24.98
Back to Basics in the Style of the Basie Band	MMO CD 3985	$19.98
Big Band Ballads: Tenor or Bass Trombone	MMO CD 3907	$19.98
From Dixie to Swing	MMO CD 3926	$19.98
Isle of Orleans	MMO CD 3933	$19.98
Jazz Standards w/Strings	MMO CD 3910	$19.98
New Orleans Classics	MMO CD 3934	$19.98
Northern Lights	MMO CD 2004	$19.98
PCH Pacific Coast Horns, vol. 1: Longhorn Serenade	MMO CD 3975	$19.98
PCH Pacific Coast Horns, vol. 2: 76 Trombones and other favs (Int-Adv)	MMO CD 3976	$19.98
PCH Pacific Coast Horns, vol. 3: Where Trombone Reigns (Int-Adv)	MMO CD 3977	$19.98
Play Ballads w/a Band	MMO CD 3972	$19.98
Standards for Trombone (Ira Lepus, trombone)	MMO CD 3935	$24.98
Studio City	MMO CD 2024	$19.98
Swing with a Band	MMO CD 3973	$19.98
Take One (minus Lead Trombone)	MMO CD 2014	$19.98
Chicago-Style Jam Session	MMO CD 3921	$19.98
Adventures in N.Y. & Chicago Jazz	MMO CD 3923	$19.98
Unsung Hero: Great Sinatra Standards	MMO CD 3906	$19.98

Laureate Master Series Concert Solos

Beginning Solos, v. I (Brevig)	MMO CD 3911	$19.98
Beginning Solos, v. II (Friedman)	MMO CD 3912	$19.98
Int. Solos, v. I (Brown)	MMO CD 3913	$19.98
Int. Solos, v. II (Friedman)	MMO CD 3914	$19.98
Advanced Solos, v. I (Brown)	MMO CD 3915	$19.98
Advanced Solos, v. II (Brevig)	MMO CD 3916	$19.98
Advanced Solos, v. III (Brown)	MMO CD 3917	$19.98
Advanced Solos, v. IV (Friedman)	MMO CD 3918	$19.98
Advanced Solos, v. V (Brevig)	MMO CD 3919	$19.98

Student Series

Classic Themes: 27 Easy Songs	MMO CD 3932	$19.98
Easy Jazz Duets 2 Trombs/Rhythm Section	MMO CD 3903	$19.98
Easy Solos: Student Level, v. I	MMO CD 3901	$19.98
Easy Solos: Student Level, v. II	MMO CD 3902	$19.98
Teacher's Partner: Basic Studies	MMO CD 3920	$19.98
Twelve Classic Jazz Standards	MMO CD 7010	$19.98
Twelve More Classic Jazz Standards	MMO CD 7011	$19.98
World Favorites: 41 Easy Selections	MMO CD 3931	$19.98

MUSIC MINUS ONE • 50 Executive Boulevard • Elmsford, New York 10523-1325 • Phone: 914-592-1188 • Fax: 914-592-3116